Bible Verse Picture Book

Jacqueline Melgren

"Commit to the Lord whatever you do, and he will establish your plans"

Proverbs 16:3, NIV

"For we live by faith, not by sight."

2 Corinthians 5:7, NIV

"Rejoice with those who rejoice; weep with those who weep."

Romans 12:15, CSB

"Even when I go through the darkest valley, I fear no danger, for You are with me;"

Psalm 23:4, CSB

"Come to Me, all of you who are weary and burdened, and I will give you rest.

Matthew 11:28, CSB

"Search for the Lord and for His strength; seek His face always."

1 Chronicles 16:11, CSB

"The LORD will fight for you; you need only to be still."

Exodus 14:14, NIV

"The Lord is my shepherd; there is nothing I lack"

Psalm 23:1, CSB

"He gives strength to the weary and strengthens the powerless."

Isaiah 40:29, CSB

"But I will restore health to you, and heal your wounds" declares the LORD

Jeremiah 30:17, NIV

"Now faith is confidence in what we hope for and assurance about what we do not see."

Hebrews 11:1, NIV

"Anxiety weighs down the heart, but a kind word cheers it up."

Proverbs 12:25, NIV

"So faith comes from what is heard, and what is heard comes through the message about Christ"

Romans 10:17, CSB

"Do everything in love."

1 Corinthians 16:14, NIV

"Therefore encourage one another and build each other up as you are already doing."

1 Thessalonians 5:11, CSB

"For God does not show favoritism."

Romans 2:11, NIV

"No one has greater love than this, that someone would lay down his life for his friends."

John 15:13, CSB

"Therefore, if anyone is in Christ, the new creation has come: The old has gone, the new is here!"

2 Corinthians 5:17, NIV

"We love because he first loved us."

1 John 4:19, NIV

"And if you believe, you will receive whatever you ask for in prayer."

Matthew 21:22, CSB

"Above all, love each other deeply, because love covers over a multitude of sins."

1 Peter 4:8, NIV

"Devote yourselves to prayer, being watchful and thankful."

Colossians 4:2, NIV

"And the peace of God, which surpasses every thought, will guard your hearts and your minds in Christ Jesus."

Philippians 4:7, CSB

"Blessed are those who mourn, because they will be comforted."

Matthew 5:4, CSB

"Indeed, we have all received grace after grace from His fullness,"

John 1:16, CSB

"A time to tear and a time to mend, a time to be silent and a time to speak,."

Ecclesiastes 3:7, NIV

"My comfort in my suffering is this: Your promise preserves my life."

Psalm 119:50, NIV

"Love must be sincere. Hate what is evil; cling to what is good."

Romans 12:9, NIV

"You will pray to Him, and He will hear you, and you will fulfill your vows."

Job 22:27, CSB

"Everything is possible to the one who believes."

Mark 9:23, CSB

CPSIA information can be obtained
at www.ICGtesting.com
Printed in the USA
BVHW020004291121
622756BV00002B/21

* 9 7 8 9 1 8 9 4 5 2 3 6 7 *